Slight

Rebecca Wolff / Slight Return / Wave Books, Seattle and New York

Return

Published by Wave Books

www.wavepoetry.com

Copyright © 2022 by Rebecca Wolff

Wave Books titles are distributed to the trade by

Consortium Book Sales and Distribution

Phone: 800-283-3572 / SAN 631-760x

Library of Congress Cataloging-in-Publication Data

Names: Wolff, Rebecca, 1967– author.

Title: Slight return / Rebecca Wolff.

Description: First edition. | Seattle : Wave Books, [2022]

Identifiers: LCCN 2022020003 | ISBN 9781950268665 (hardcover)

ISBN 9781950268658 (paperback)

Subjects: LCGFT: Poetry.

Classification: LCC PS3623.O56 S58 2022 | DDC 811/.6—dc23/eng/20220425

LC record available at https://lccn.loc.gov/2022020003

Printed in the United States of America

9 8 7 6 5 4 3 2 1

First Edition

Wave Books 103

1

2

I think of people who say that setting your guitar on fire has nothing to do with the music as cellophane, bags and bags of cellophane. Of cellophane but in bags of cellophane. Have you ever thought of lighting cellophane on fire? There's no need to.

www.rollingstone.com/music/music-news/jimi-hendrix-1942-1970-93969

1

The character of something

the more you listen to it—emerges. Blue

blue, blue, blue
hydrangea

in the shade. *Blue, blue, blue, blue*
hydrangea. If he could be happy without me I

would leave him there

instantaneously. Dehydrated box
of box turtle deserving your censure. "Me minus you" is

a terrapin homestead,
sales encrypted,
sales diamondback *sails*

sales—*sails*—is that what you were trying to tell me, "sails"?
normal speaking voice in tones like consensus on the air when
no one is there there is nothing more intersubjective

than that. We eat

at the same time. Ugly

in the light of day, frontal
in the shade—vibrationally agonistic—

deterministic as a brindle decahedron.

experiment in voice and character #1

I dressed carefully for the [ ]

I dressed carefully, a loaded gun.

I dressed carefully, choosing my weapon

I dressed recklessly for the [single most important day of my life]

I dressed recklessly, in a uniform [ ]

I dressed carefully, with intention, for the day was warm and I
    was to be married

I dressed carefully that single most important day of my life
    without intention

"I care so much for you and that is it."

Experiment in Divination: Voice and Character

There is a curiosity that knows
I know

deathless ceiling of unknowing
I know

Querent,

Who I ask
is changing

all the time

changing
now changed.

How else is one to know
How is one to know how to proceed

course of action

a nonreflective surface

playing card on a picnic table
a knot of knowing on a node of playing

How is one to know
How else is one to know how to proceed

How is one to make a motion against—

electric word life

and there's forever
and that's a mighty long time.

experiment in voice and character #3

and that's a feeling you can only have alone

and that's a feeling you can only have alone

and that's a feeling you can only have alone

I'm going home to see my Jesus

That boy is dead and gone.

Experiment in Voice and Character:
"In the absence of general literacy"

The bad habit

really takes you
away from
everything that matters

sleep behind
sunglasses

if no sleep you can
drink water

why couldn't I sleep?
Because I couldn't
spell. Incant or querent or trance.

Why I can't talk to you

anymore. You really—
in my sleep deprived—
on a rolling
train to the city to learn to deal, to spread—
the cards.

You really, so emphatic, I cannot emphasize

enough you really
are the only one I've ever—

oh and now I've found you
again there
in my water

glass.
Declaiming in my small cave
of a mouth

occulted learning
there is no effort to be made too grandstanding

I will speak with you again.

Experiment: Institutional Critique

I was not able to be
myself

Public
muttering

is discouraged by public.
Publicly muttering

not literally but publicly you understand
that's three times removed, that's

hearing what I would say if I said it; hearing what I say when I
don't really say it; hearing and thinking about what it would
sound like if I said it and I meant it; my

son told me yesterday he can't view himself from the outside, he
can only see himself inside but he also can't see anybody else,
he can only see himself, and only inside. It's the only self he has
and he can't see anybody else. I can see myself only from the out-
side, and I can see everyone else from the outside too. I know
exactly what the outside of everything looks like, including my-
self, and this is why they follow me around taking snapshots of
my style and putting it on TV, selling it to the masses only five
days after I actually rocked that outfit, old Irish sweater with

the elbows worn to holes, now on sale at Anthropologie. They follow me from where I live to where I choose to live next and they sell it to the upper classes. And the masses suffer because of my inexorable and unerring sense of what will be cool in the institution. The institution will be cool with my style.

You can have it. You can't have it. You can't have it because you bought it. You bought it and you

ruined it. I ruined it by being myself;

I was not able to be myself because you bought it. That's not a good example, let me find another example. Nightclubbing in the '80s. Shape of my ass. Shape of my eyebrows, shape of my long, long fingers. Romanticism. People struggling with how to get outside their head. Reconciling their head with the cloud. The other cloud. Their other head.

The Narrative of Their Execution/
The Execution of Their Narrative

I didn't see it, so I know it's not there. I looked all over for it,
    and I didn't see it. It definitely wasn't there.

I can rock that look.
I can rock that look. I can

rock
that
look.
I can   and have

rocked
that look.

2

On Sunday I Water the Plants

Just joking my days are chaotic
the way I like them
these lines are demon-
strative

but a week is a round
number

a week is measured in days and there are seven
just like the fingers on my hands without those ones I

forget, chopped off, bitten off, fell off from scurvy and flesh-
eating: intentionally brutal. Painfully severe. Tens of

thousands of extremes
in the medium

daily.
Every day. Every
single day.

if I were more orderly

the extraction of value,
attachment to intention

10,000 orderlies

if I were a hospital orderly
mucking out the stall

of permaculture
dating myself
10,000 enthusiasms

10,000 maniacs

poop into a bucket
water the poop make tea
pour the tea on the kale experiment
so far it is all going according to plan

avocado in the salad
shell of avocado in the compost
fruit flies in the wine bath

the cryptic coming back you all understand me.

I don't know do you love me even crazy? *what does* crazy *mean.*
  Do you love me
even bad. *what does* bad *mean.*

I murdered someone. I just want to say that at the outset
flat out

side of the head with a shovel or pickax, something blunt but
  sharp: corpse overboard.
and then I lied about it
worse made art about it

she drowned hit her head on a stump

and then worse

I told a lot of people what I had done
sheer hubris

processing the head
cheese like Melissa
Sue Anderson or like Melissa
Gilbert; or any Melissa—spending a whole day smashing

processing
a pumpkin, the guts and the meat, the seed.

I am the _____

It is wearing, to go it alone

but g-d gave me the str-ng-h

make
a foray into village
into villagers

hooray gave me the *strength*

to understand a poem no problem

formal gift from language diode, diadem, overgloss, subslime.
    That's not a typo that's an
egregious coinage minted in a prideful cataract.

I am the tooth fairy, G-d
gave me the str-ng-h to slip

under a heavy pillow   extract a sharp
credulous

molar and to part

with my ten

dollar

poem:
no problem: on a scale of one

ten is the shape of the poem and the voltage why
and the hidden context that makes it all right

the content without which

we would all die. On

top of that all the desperate measures repose:
dandelion greens or wine picked fresh, bacterium home-
grown callous or casual

who is inner,
man, you choose who is inner.

Objective Reality Can Take Care of Itself

I have no problem

—the interpersonal

a supernatural episode—

her phone got
      lost

inside a comfy chair. Deep down inside. Natural

light in short supply but that is
not a reflection on me personally—

it's the window and the air and the sounds.
I only hang out with people

who are psychic
anything else is a

waste of precious

continuity. I

can do what I want
with this whole day: Does that make me

feel any better? Relief
from pressure
to comply, FOMO get
lost the great

outdoors, does it make me
objectively better.

Like all my enthusiasms

ten thousand enthusiasms

and anyone who thinks they love me
needs to listen to the radio if they want
to understand me

it's no consolation

to be psychic I want you to

say it to my face
I command you to say it to my face

thus the poem is a spell
like it was a throne

In the name of all that is a name
and has a name

black cat sleeping in my face on my pillow
formed to me
morphed to me
breathing into my face

the moon traveling quickly
ever more visible

objects of name
named in a spell

three moons imbued with energetic
with magnetic
invested in the power in me

and literal
pressed to my sternum where the heart
beats visibly

like Captain
Beefheart says I don't make
music   I make what seems plain to me

plain to anybody else
and that is how attachment to content—
attachment IS content—
detachment to surface
all buzzwords
in my heart. Come live in my heart

and be my love. I am not quoting

I am ironizing and by ironizing I am

intoning or invoking, the word that means:
"saying it in a magical way" that is not the common
form of utterance: it's a heightened form
of utterance that means I give it meaning and that meaning
    then transposes: it divinely

attaches to the gods up in the heavens
mount Olympus

thank heavens it attaches
the attachment of meaning is divine and I can do it
with my heart

my visible heart
makes me a god   Thus in ecstasy

I think you can see.

Raga You Bet

There is no irony with which

I apprehend this ancient cultural
wisdom

materially accessible to me
just because on my couch I can

access on my iPhone
from iTunes

it yet goeth round

and round
it yet sootheth and stirreth

old-timey motherfucker
thank you

eternally George

Harrison who in your young
wisdom, wisdom

of youth and with the excessive wealth

you found
in musicianship, accessed

and Anglicized and befriended truly and wholly
without irony

as you lived
and breathed. There is no such irony

and no more
irony

like the irony with which I approach
your ancient
youth and truth and death.

The Big Pic Is a Total Art Shot

High-def selfie in the sunstroke glass that conveniently
frames and reflects. Making art

I'm so lithe I'm a fuckin'

sylph. Then on the floor not a moment
later child's pose

right another abject
tableau of lineation: enjamb
those long
limbs   a cave

for a dim little self to make dim
little faces. Oh no

I'm learning from my students. This pose *Oh no*

I'm done with mastery, that leaves big old me
sadly free

of all immunity. *But how* ... —   Butter
is a food group in the Old Country, bread

too sour for belief. It's rye, it's unbelievable. Anti-

depressants a food, a group, here in the Oldlands, a cave. *But
how can you*: ... —Every

thing disorganizes once you leave
mastery behind, it's not a mystery, it's mastery, or is that
   when, is that time, or space. You're on the floor you're in the
   window You're just like

everybody else. *But how can you* without self-

congratulation? I'm just literally going to follow
this river to find my way back to the center. There is literally
   a gas truck in my path excruciatingly
slowly backing up. Beep   beep   beep   beep. Repeat repeat
   you're just like
everybody else repeat repeat
you're just like every-
body else. Fuck that snowflake in its bal-

-lerina asshole it will melt.

Scales have fallen from my eyes

Celebrate
History
Month

the whiteness
of paradigm

shift
mission drift

I have never fixed to learn anything

knit
purl
knit
purl
purl the knits
knit the purls

it knits itself and wears itself
it sells itself and buys itself: it is a fabric
I am the engine of Kali

what is Kali, western civilization? Kali is not a metaphor
Get in there with the image and the action of
Kali. Intellection

is appropriation
I am writing this no more
for myself than I am writing this
for you

I am writing this no more for myself.

Then I am writing this for you—longer lines more gracious—

And this is where the missionaries come in, they come in
volunteering

Their mission is not clear, their mission is clear.

The Singing Revolution

Paneriai Memorial, Vilnius, Lithuania

You may approach that stone
You may sit here,
see here.
See from here.

How can I sing about
not that optimal
distance

but *about*? Wd that

in a wood
be desirable? Rhyme
or reason: everyone
has a
reason—Systematic
evil in the past.

Tune of Reason = removed from empathic of course because
    reason is

a closed system: within a pit. Or is it opposite? Reason

must be ratified by consensus? Reason is bounded
    psychologically, or Reason is

unbound on a scale of Realism. Reason a vector that marches
    fearlessly out: And Rhyme

a bubble, bounded ephemera. No, yes, it is Rhyme that allows

empathic coalition ... Meanwhile, the guide in effective English

describes exertions in the pit and the manner in which the
    columns filed
collapsed into the trenches
of the pit describes

describes. "not only to the pit
but in trenches" that is described

in notes in bottles
buried
in the garden. Semantic

Genocide? I dunno how many. How many does it take. Dramatic
    irony guide
tells how

meticulous note-taker was shot for bicycle
one week in advance of liberation. Backward glance at the evil in
    the past

Backward glance at scale of massive human pit through the
    tall, tall trees: "Oooph,

another pit"

—and we pushed the guide into the pit.

The Lens of Porcelain

For example,
one of many lenses
one of many ways
to look.

An idea I brought to bear
and it failed
or with some degree of success
it "worked"
tentacle magic
it materially
changed
the condition it wrapped around.

This is your wake-up call, over
and over and
wake up again
and wake up again
and wake up
again
opening the lid
it's not the same lid
every time
the lid
is a little different.

It wrapped around
a space that was a
context:

likeness of daffodil. Discriminating
or making a hierarchy
is just the beginning
of our shared

sum. What "we" equal. You have a lens
and a sum. You have objective
calculations and subjective
choices to make about
which of the many
of the many

I'll try this another
way. Habits of mind
are just habits
to be broken like any
other. Paradigms
are habits. A chair
is a seat of being: a big
position you're sitting on. "That's a big"
position you've got there, a contraption
attached like an optometrist's diagnostic
tool for lens assessment. For seeing

what "we" see. Subscribing. Subscription
to a lens requires
fixed address, attachment to position. Attachment is a kind of
   subscription.
Subscribe today to my
love my *life* my *heart* my *mind*
subscribe to the tool I made
for seeing. With this lens I thee

mirage
I thee phantasm
I thee fix I thee nurture
with slight

return. With exposition
of position no other than *from*
and *to*. I can't help it

lens makes sense.

Slight Return

I'm living backwards I'm so delayed

But
I have been given the opportunity to begin again
to start over, moving forwards

bereft, stripped bare, bereaved, the old

personality wasn't working and nothing meant anything anymore,
   the old meaning apparatus
did not produce meaning anymore:

I've been given an opportunity to start over

sound familiar— (How *can* a person be)

I'm going to have to look for something else
to give my life meaning

to give meaning to my life; as for continuing, one must

or is it possible to decide to continue no matter what, vessel?
    and then you just do the *every day, every day* thing—

It is a good thing there is so much time in the day
each day hours for each trespass

hallowed and
valorized,

vaporized.

3

Corrective: A Companion

The demands of art
        upon my art

—full cognizance
—full digitized

Whale's blow, rich and foul
        as "fathoms deep"

And rain it mingles
        with the tears
upon my cheek.

Artful behavior:

Toe-to-heel backward
        steep up
Gospel Path

Beeline to hermitage
        screens aflame
with all that's passed

What's with the arid ground

around the Louvre?
Yellow sandy soil like Arizona.
It is one of many entrances
trampled underfoot. Outside the modern artist
Inside the artists have been making and made

and continue to make a grand statement
and to capture
within l'histoire
the shape
of the content
of some dead angel
undying.

She is on a pedestal no less we look up her skirts.
I would like to join the long line
to come to know into.

Did somebody wait all their lives
dream all their days
to arrive in this large space

Did someone just jump for joy
in front of the camera,
back to

the angel?

Go into the square of art's mistake
and jump for joy for the camera.

context is everything

and in this one I am a witch

so what if I ingested the vapors
of heavy
metals, available to my nervous
system
through my nostrils, pores, mouth, hair

and ride a bicycle insensate
prey and prone
cray and crone

John Ashbery has already met
his timely end

at the courthouse
catty-corner the village green.

From there I ride to the landscape
witch of the East
come late for the tour, the house
tour

and find the tour departed, unjoinable.

From a distance the shapes the river takes untrammeled

overall the general feeling
from the viewshed
is I am being poisoned and
I am poison

where is the nuance for that?

Marshall McLuhan said his piece
his pieces. Medium,

the message, warlock, contour, warrior.

That's not how my imagination works

It is sovereign

always has been

I like to steal things, sometimes

from my enemies. Too big

to fail, not too big

to fail: I am stepping

down to spend more time

with my family. I will work

for food. Flipping

through the conversations archived and un-
archived—we have no use for this kind of advanced
thinking anymore. Having failed
on the basic levels. Bottoms up: don't let poison
poison you. Don't let
poison
poison me.

Austerity Rabbit Cage

Austerity is not the case
for rabbits they desire

and will find fuzzy
bits

chew willow
till it splits

seek empathy
what is the ... (word for head that sees only on one side):

"it's called ... a ... 'victim.'"
sidereal eye-view

monocular
hide empathy till it splits
the binary.

It happens a rabbit will never go home.
They make of your home

a rabbit zone a
box for living an

Empathy box.
Rabbits can I sit with you inside

Rabbits turn and see the other side

Will you disassociate with me?

The essential weakness of my character is evident in the struc-
ture of my face. It is mimetic. Phylogeny replicates ontology or
something ringing in my ears periodically all my life. It is evident
in the structure of my sentences. The essential strengths of my
character are evident in the bones of my face. High and mighty
brought low over and over and over. Bend over baby, not just
anything is worth writing.

About my legs. About legs. Historic legs; constructive legs, un-
impeachable legs, superlative legs. The lens of legs. Legs they
wanna see. Legs give them something to talk about. Legs all the
way to heaven. How you observe them. How you measure them.

Could you have guessed
that I care about aesthetics from the way I [ ]. The way I choose
    not to include

Standing in the doorway open to the backyard on a civic alley
    my own fitness mocks me.

My fitness mocks me. Time makes you bolder even children get
    older

The way I walk is just the way I walk.

+++

I wake up with a song called Passionate Fools in my head; it is a cheesy late eighties television theme song of my own invention. My head invented it in my sleep.

I woke up not knowing what "intersectionality" means and needing to use the internet to find out. I owe the internet a big debt, a favor, a debt of gratitude. I owe you a favor, what can I do for you, Internet. Payback is not the same as empathy but we take what we can get and give and get.

+++

It's hard to get post-irony
I feel for you
I think I love you. *That's not funny.*

Tragedy, like racism, is systemic. There is no such thing as a
  personal
tragedy—oxymoronic. You and me babe; our tragedy. When it
  ceases to be tragic

to you that's my tragedy alone and then it's
no comedy either, I am loser hear me roar. Having put to bed

forever the sense that everything will be

all right, now we proceed toward whatever referent.

+++

Doting fan of synchronicities, or deluded victim—victim I say—
of concentric models in which I am centric. Not centrist or ec-
centric but centric, and the radio talks to me and the songs in-
dividually have messages for me and the weather responds to
my needs and glorifies, sometimes characterizes me. All these
are available and understood diagnostically and philosophically,
everyone is looking at me. A revelation to understand that at
least it is patently untrue that everyone is looking at me, every-
one is concerned with my status or situation or who I am going
to sit next to at the dinner table at the art colony. Everyone,
child, listen to me, *everyone is far too concerned with who they are
going to sit next to at the dinner table at the art colony to spare even
one moment.*

+++

In this poem I reveal

prostrate myself before

an essential weakness in my character

cloaked

as a bearing
position
load-bearing

pinion
or sturdy element

The situation can be described thusly:

my animals and partners serve
as test cases or study groups—focus groups

I am subject
they are conditions

For example this morning I stood on my deck above the yard in back. The cats had been let out and they were down there moaning and groaning at the neighbor's cat. I talked to them. I called them. I called them by their names and they looked up at me, surprised—they did not know that I knew their names so well.

They paused, arrested.

I watched as they responded. I observed their response to my ministrations of their names and said them further in cooing tones.

They arched their backs in pleasure and coiled around, gave up their morning spat. Rose up the stairs, gold eyes in the green morning, watching me, and lay around on the landing and thumped their tails, aimlessly, preening a bit in pleasure at my attention.

This is how I should have loved my babies.

This is how I should love you now. I learned it in an experiment
on my cats.

Political Animals

I am of the 2%
We do not speak casually to our pets
Mine endure my silence
They warble all day for food even though I feed them
just fine—clearly they are looking
for something else
from me—humans call it love
Psychologists call it attachment
Relational psychologists call it relation.
Today— ... I am so sick of the structure given to me for
    telling
my stories. It goes: I am here,
sitting in a chair on a special day. It is finally getting cold out,
winter 2017, when will people stop
telling me it's a beautiful day, it's not beautiful if it's
    poisoned.
71 degrees in November. One black cat
settles in my lap—this is not unusual, not
a story worth the centering of my self. She
is the little sister lap cat. Do you
post pictures of your cats

or dogs all day every day? Well
then I unfollow you. Today
I am sitting in a chair, having forced myself
to stay here long enough for these creatures

I live with

to find me trust me experience time passing and me staying
    still. They

only see me standing still when I am standing

glued to my phone

scrolling in a state

of doped paralysis, you heard me,

there's nothing good going on there

you are being drugged, roped

and branded this is no joke. I am

here in my chair to tell you.

In my lap the first cat, little

sister, who every day steps aside from her meal with bits to
    spare

on her plate for her big fat

brother, steps aside in a way I have

interpreted as sisterly,

her concern her care her love

for her brother, she also licks him clean when

he stands still for it,

today it's cold enough

and he climbs up on the chair

to suss out a spot

next to her in my lap. A first. He uses his whiskers

and other devices

to calibrate and calculate depth, exactly

how much space-time he needs

determines the angle of recline

and now I have two black cats in my lap
sleeping
while I read a review of a book
on the poet Czesław Miłosz's long-buried critique
of Americans, the regular kind, and also American
intellect and intellectuals,
and how they are bought/

sold, the bubble of consumption
that makes them sleep/

keeps them from waking. Brother
cat shifts and heaves his bulk
encroaches a bit on sister's
spot, I feel dangerous

in my lap, sister
feels it too, rises up,
hisses like a boss.
Her blood runs
colder than I thought. These
kingdoms
take the cake. There is no more
tension to break—they resettle, sleep as one
as long as I hold still. My
needs soon
make me move.

Hallowe'en

and in the bar I met a witch she was our waitress
she spoke casually of ceremony
up to her chin in water to protect her
channeling the dead, speaking to the dead, they speak *through* her
her sore throat after

her mother and her mother's mother also channeled
the dead, when she reached a certain age her mother said to her
"I see them too"—and the waitress's eyes are like
no other eyes I've ever seen but they remind me
of your eyes

your dead mother's eyes you received them
I've never seen them

—soon departed—

she leaves our table my friend
tells me that he knew her a while back. Profane life
in Brooklyn, she doesn't remember that they met—

he tells me that she told him that every day
she stares at the sun for ten minutes and for that reason
he doesn't like her—it is not good for you, everyone
knows that and within two or three years if she keeps

doing that she will go blind. I don't understand the way
the things he says make sense within the context
of her

enchantment. I could see why she would stare
at the sun. I remember the eclipse only
a few summers ago where everyone, everyone with eyes was
    enjoined
to look at the sun through a handmade box
and only afterward was I given to understand
by someone I trust with
arcana
that this was a grave misstep
uncontained energies unleashed widely in the world
nothing has been right ever since
but nothing was right before
I visually in my memory
gaze and my eyes feel it

and after we get the check I see in the dim
rural bourgeois bar at each table
a rainbowing, gaseous haze refracting each flame, rays glazing
    the ocular
darkness in the corner
of my eye that means a migraine coming on.
I need to get home, lie down, close my eyes. When I try to see
myself with love through someone who loves me's eyes
it makes me weep. So lit,
unchained and undead.

The supernatural

is a metaphor
for love

The super
natural
is a metaphor
for love

all I know is
you like it when I talk to you directly
I address directly
you

you like it
now I know that
I know that to be true
I won't forget it
another thing
I'll do for you

I'll remember
you are real,

yes I do.

4

rock heart

weak heart

baby heart

brokenheart

fucked hot

I saw you this morning

I saw you drowning

I saw you this morning

you raised your hand to me obscurely
as would a prisoner from behind bars
salute the laws and customs and the fresh, obscure desires
    that put him there

wraparound picket fence obscuring your view
and literally you could not see all of me at once

as with this forge Emily Dickinson spoke of there is no
    distinction to be made here

between the literal and the symbolic, it's all one all the time
all one here now in your head and mine

you took my heart I'll never stop saying it
it's on your property with you

This was almost more excitement

than my
heart could bear

This was almost too intense—
I cried out—

This was almost more engagement
than my heart knew—
how to—

gave out
10 stiff little fingers
clenching

and unclenching

jigsaw puzzle on the table

Betty Grable
Julian Schnabel

historically we as a people
have proved able

withstanding so much torment

or torpor

and "move on"

This = This

Triple crème is Saint-André
zucchini, gigantic chunks

I need to know how to communicate my preferences to you

how to communicate with you
Now that we are on this planet disturbed. I need to talk to you
and there is no way to talk to you, but you are not dead. Conun-

drum. How can it be with all this

technology

There is no way I can "reach out"
There is no fucking way I can talk to you

but I still fucking love you. Now,

if you want to be rid of me,

get rid of me. But if you want to
get free of me

well then

be free of me.

There Is Nothing Like a Good Shit

And it doesn't stop
there

my dream,
That I walked beside him beside

his wife, he gripped
my hand unknown
to her

Up Close & Personal

It's illustrative what comes out of a
face,

you get that close, what goes into yours,
motes and shrapnel,

makes hearts pound
your face an atomizer

all base
reduced

to infant sense:
his odor wronged

yours is the face. I can't

let go I just can't let go all I dream about is the arena in her
    hair, your wife's luxuriant hair, that mess at the back she
    wore to the party maybe you fucked that mess into her hair.

head injury in the arena

last night's kind meal, agape with panacea, only the right
    person is right. only the right person

is right for me otherwise I am alone all right. I have a million
    friends. Some

make the others look like enemies. Some of them with
    piercing gaze and
perspicacious heart; I'm hubristic so it requires

a dagger to my heart

put it in.

Cheerful whistling of the kettle

Total devastation
complete disorder
completely
demoralized, totally demoralized

I couldn't see colors
I couldn't hear music—
they belonged to you

But thank god somebody was listening when the '90s
and all the electric, whatever that was that was going on with
    that low,
downbeat, and the voice cast over, echo chamber, thank god
    somebody was

whistling.

Why do you inspire

Why are you the only
it is not for art

it is not for the passing of time
it is not for the refuge

it is not for the synchronicity the radio dj
the theme of "coming home to you"

it is not only so I can say it
it is not for the purposes of art I repeat

it is so I can experience: urgency
it is all for me?

it is not because I need to feel that I am at the center
of a grand scheme; that's not why

You inspire voluntarily or transitively
intransigently

Why don't you stop inspiring—this is rhetorical—don't listen
   to me
never stop please

I have to answer the question once and for all is it the real "you."
Someone keeps asking me that over and over

and will not let me love you or know how to love you until I
    provide a definitive
the proof

It is not an agency

Clouds rafters beams roof sky meeting of scaffold and brace and
    bracket:
I located you from a picture you transmitted.

Peak Experience

Having successfully dismantled former apparatus

I was never a fantasy
I have always been real as fuck.
And how I wield a cliché

tells you a lot about a person

appetite for husbands
other women's husbands

I can see other women's husbands

a mile away. This one's a grown man.

He can like my shit on Instagram.

And even my heart doesn't matter

huge heart for you
my heart hard as a rock for you
direct address to you from this rock hard heart

Dismantle that, dreamy

nook I got you in there, enlarged and glaring
come out you are no bigger than
I am no bigger than

The things that aggrandize
are all the things we write about and sing about

the things that make distinctions are all the art parts
the politics come out of our heart parts.

Okay, so

It is still to be revealed

can you live with that?

what will be my salvation

somber and joyful
shakes and shudders
when I touch him

Minus the Supernatural

With my beautiful friend I'm in a restaurant, Korean, farm-to-table joint. Bibimbap and pork fried rice, cocktails with Suja, grapefruit, hemlock. I used to hate poems that named places: this went down in Troy, New York.

She's been sharing with me, I've been sharing with her, we share an obsessive relationship to love flown far away, hers to Ojai. Mine in terms like Red Flags Fly. We neither of us, my friend and I relate,

ever cease checking our phones, check the magic of thinking that every minute is just another minute in which he may appear, however unlikely. In my case I've been explicitly told he won't. Won't return to me, won't return my love. It's a tight

rat-like snatch at synaptic blancmange, by which rats
might be satisfied but never are, don't have to be, a taste only
makes more habit. Snapshot (obsolete) 2017: If my lost love
     posts

a shot of a lit-up library at dusk, or his black silhouette in a
     forest, tbt
he's grey now—the modernity of it all kills me—slays me—I hate
     this kind of poem—

it's not for me, the shot, it's for everybody, everybody plus the
   bots, plus the hundred
rando Aussie lifestyle thots.

She gets up to get us more drinks. We've come to a place that
   feels
raw and red-eyed, ferreted, may reform
ourselves through sharing. I mean to continue the dialogue in
my head, talk to myself about my phone in my pocket rather than
reach into my pocket, extract my phone: he's texted me, I think,
synapse charge, power surge, then I think

No, Rebecca, he hasn't
that cheap habit you have of magical thinking, that's gotten you in
a lot of trouble: the kind nobody needs, nobody needs to think magi-
cally of him, he's not worth it, he's not magic like that, and the narra-
tive in which you and he are magically connected and speak to each
other telepathically with your hearts, well that's a stagnant tragic
comedy of error, a hyperindividualistic binge watch starring you and
you alone. My hand in my pocket I withdraw

to look, and look again: he has.

Reincarnations

upon the ground

and in this life—
yes this lifetime to see again—
you rose again—

and sealed lip
to ear
sealed line of lip—

entry to ear of love.
Inside the
loved.

＊

So much weird ice
everywhere and on the ground

Human error everywhere
good nutrition everywhere

at the bottom—scraping the

bottom,
value-

added, all abuse
is born of worry—Antabuse—

is structure, really.
You rose again—

    *

that's how I
manage my anxiety
that's how I know you'll

come for me

I did not ask for this
supernatural
sense of things

Class Clown

In the dark of night

I left my home (I live
alone). Up at 4 to catch Delta 6
twenty-five—drive

through the dark
brights on. Parking Level P3
Column 44, hot radiation
pagoda, one may elect
instead to use a female. "Use of This Technology
Is Optional." I opt
for human hands, opt
to use yr woman hours, gentle female
expertise, and nonthreatening. Nothing
to see here, move along, fellow
travelers. Female,
pat me down, swift touch, blue latex
fingers: I will feel around your

waistband now with the backs
of my hands. These are the backs
of my hands you are feeling now at the join
of groin and thigh, light
touch. Now you're going to feel me

at your breast: that's the back
of my hands. I am a little high

already, relaxed, bereft, .5 mg of Xanax
washed down in the parked car
water purified at my kitchen
tap in the middle of the night, PUR water filter, green
indicator light indicating
filtration, salvation, overdetermination.

The first leg in my sleep, crooked
neck, drool, passive
transformation. Layover
two hours. In a leather recliner
I await the thing I want, my game, this aesthetician, licensed,

to trim my cuticles, lacquer
my nails vermilion. Unseat
me. While I wait
this patented XpresSpa chair miracle does the work

of a licensed
masseuse: firm pressure rolling
under my weight expertly, tirelessly, *amazing human*, symmetrical
along the symmetrical
muscles supporting my spine, firm
human pressure from living balled-up fists
that live inside the leather, that

inexhaustibly
apply
firm
pressure.

Katelyn is a history buff.
Air force brat in the airport
spa, she's never flown
anywhere. Nowhere. She likes to learn
about things, she says, the
things
that happened and you can
find out weird stuff about
them. She is taking great pains
with my fingers. I find out, weirdly, how
lucky I really am, with my inexhaustible liberal

arts education and equipoise, critical
apparatus and layers, grids, volume-free
rubric of speechless apprehension I received
from the library. Would you unseat
me? I mention
to Katelyn libraries,
card catalogs, she is currently into
the *Titanic*. Katelyn says *I can recall
the smell of books*: When she was a child
her father would take her
to the Barnes & Nobles [sic], where he

would read up on history. Back then she was into
arts 'n' crafts. Hours 'n' hours,
she tells me, I am agog, how she still
recalls the "smell of the books, all the new books." She is
nostalgic. Titanic. She does a terrible

job on my nails—you never know what you will get,
what you paid for, should all her training
pay off—they are splintered and distressed, she has filed
against the grain, they are squared and gloppy, she has colored
outside the lines, I thank her and tip her
profusely. I have been made

late for boarding and sprint lightly
along the moving
walkway to Terminal C. Paging Passenger
Rebecca Wolff.

I know what I'll do I'll pretend you're dead,

so literal,
revise my memoir to include
the irredeemable

losses,
so real as to be visible
your death to me
I used to say

you were dead to me

rigid like foamcore
inflexible unlike
the synthetic fibers
growing out of
Joni
Mitchell's
arm pores but

what can I do when the whole world
pushes off
the whole world waves cheerio
in a skiff and I

gyrate unprettily on the shore

it is my selfishness

it is my self-centeredness

it is what I can't see

it is the end of me

more poems about

how bad I am

this was meant to be a poem about how I wish I could speak
    with you

and how I will have to learn to truly do without

this is the first unpoem

I am always trying to amuse you

The polis
no substitute
mouth breather, blank as compared
to you, can it be true I had one

correspondent
audience
only one to try to please. It's the way
religious
people feel—one god one mercy one flowering
of the word.
Is everyone else a people pleaser, trying to please everyone else?
   I don't give a fuck

(about anyone else)
and there are those who appreciate that
about me. Watch me while I
work
watch me work
not giving a fuck

the question of audience
it comes up frequently
on a panel
reconstituting

the greater good
watch me work

like an organist athletically treading,
exertion steady,
pedals producing a muted hoot throughout a large cathedral
big noise roofed or unroofed, the roof blown off or burned off
from the inside, a nest of bees bespoke inside and used to
smoke—unfazed by smoke, the bees rehome.

All that matters is I work. The one I speak to is you and not you.
No one cares what shows you watch. The shared experience of
drugged commitment to viewing is only sharing rape—
eye-rape ear-rape receptor-rape synapse-rape—your consent to
entries thus coerced. Multiple entrances, one sweet meatsack.
And when the 5G planet gets all lit
infant penguins drowned, it appears to me mercifully, we should
all be drowned so mercifully in the unsack of molten glacier, sack
let loose under the cloud so we can stream more games—of
thrones, of chance, of up-close personal first-person sharing—
This concludes our nightly broadcast.

Yet another perfect example
of how it's not all about me

I say *example* instead of demonstration
I say "perfect" in the air
to demonstrate that I know for once and for all

for good and for the greater good

that it is bee season

the swarm Lucy and I just witnessed—
enhanced chronological—first we thought midges high in the
    air in a cone-
shaped flotilla
then heard the drone, concerted humming, a buzzing against
    the moan
of the Gloucester foghorn, and saw the hive loose but in
    formation in the air, released

to do no harm
Lucy's fear—
that they could smell her fear—
unanswered

and just the other day I was in my bed, it was morning, it was
    first thing.

I heard a ticking or chipping, a clicking or scratching. The bee
was large and angry looking somehow, unstable, angry to have
     alit
on a corduroy wedge pillow on the floor where I sit
sometimes to reconnect with
consensuality, my heart in my breast and what it asks for from
     the "world." The bee
wobbling on a corduroy ridge and I contained it under a jar,
     slid an envelope beneath and released it
on the porch. How on earth
did it get inside, I still do not know to this day. A minor
mystery, not even
synchronicity. But later that day

I went out for a run and as I loped under a drooping arch of
     branch, some bush, maybe forsythia, its buds long dropped—
darned if some other bee did not inject me with its venom for no
     reason. On the spot
on my arm where long ago, at least forty years of imprecision, I
     received an injection of some toxin, a vaccine with two or
     maybe three
anti-

bodies suspended in preservatives and media—the kind that no
one really knows what it will do to all of us, it is too soon—no
one/ everyone/ totalizing/ reducing. Growing and shrinking/ eat
me drink me/ save me/ say the bees—

5

Institutional Memory: check your head

Who cares
what is in a marriage

The snowy owls
and the barn owls

wiry wolves wrassling
in the snow drifts
of our protectorate

the family
is an institution

you've got the old days
in your hand

the snow days

the golden glow days

Can you perform the husband duty for me
and check

my head for lice

That is what it is in a marriage

now we will not be together when we grow older
and older but we will do it

just the same

Protecting my interests

She said you have to protect your interests.

If I were to murder my ex-husband
and destroy myself as well
this would be the note you'd find

silence
silence and
and whatever mind of winter.

My children's lawyer said "Hate ages you; don't hate, hate
    ages you"

She's wrong: Hate doesn't allow you to age properly, hate
    freezes the part of you that hates, you need to let your hate
    age with you, that's how to properly hate.

What you have to do *you have to do some*
soul-

searching
it means

interpretive dance of wild
lilies

another mound
under which

in my heart you are no longer
living. What is the best revenge?

Redistribution of your ill-got gains

and with complete transparency
I see how deep
my interests
how deeply embedded

with the broadcast
and with the information about them

how deep my interests go
the voice wipes it out. Voice

recognition—in all the wrong places,
in the sky   lord in the sky.

It is my lack of judgment that has given me the conviction.
Now I have to make

better choices
it is my lack of conviction that makes me such a poor judge.

In your recent campaign against me

you have had at every step the complicity
of the patriarchy
and you should be ashamed of yourself.

Also know
that if I found you

already

dead lying in a ditch

I would not make the effort necessary to turn you over
and hide your face

carrion
or from the sun. These are the environments

of our grievances

now you are welcome to my deepest
unwelcome

feelings

eat them like a bird eats
your face.

An Insult to Biology

This mutuality
how you hiss at me on the phone your expletives
how I relish
the brutality of prefiguring: partially severing
your head from your body—particular

arteries, slicing
motion of my blade. How ruthlessly I would

move. For we

have made our children
they live on the earth and are its last hope

and your DNA and my phenotype and the work
of our blood constricting—they live together.

It's like
lice, persistent
metaphor. Our daughter's
head, hospitable
to them. They cross from one home to another,
riding the carrier. You don't know how
to see the seed-like
silver eggs or their flat,

hair-colored bodies. They turn themselves
sideways. It takes hours
to sit and patiently, lovingly, decipher each nit
from each long strand of teenage hair. She's
afraid to ask you to do this, and afraid to ask you
to let me do this. Because

of your monstrous implication. Don't

you see the heads will roll
continuously. Don't you see
the chopping block. You can't chop
off someone's head to rid them of lice. You have to pick
the eggs off with your fingers and put them in a bowl of soapy
water. They drown. And then you drink it. That

is how to rid a darling head of lice.

My Lawyer Said That I Should Call Her

If I was visited by a ghost in the night and changed
my mind—   Executive

functioning in highest
order. The ghost comes, sits, says, in what tongue, in language
   I can understand. She says I'm sick of poems. Verse for the
   living. She knows

I only speak to ghosts now, only ghosts talk to me, when I
   speak to myself it is in ghost

I speak   I conceived

I married loved died in that order and from the top
down, when I weep I weep at the thought

of the pressure of tears behind
my eyes, at the thought of tears in the eyes

of my child at the sight of a ghost

I was, objectively, a happier person,
when I was with you.

You have had great successes in your life
in another sense you are a failure

from afar or close up:
failure or success
it is a question of scope and perspective

dry and wet terminology
am I alive
you tell me

wake up thoroughly
animist
murmuring to all creatures

stupid and evil like most or many
In the grand scheme

what does it matter if I am a bad
person? I am just one bad person. The end

of narcissism.

I find if I say it aloud into my voice
recorder I have no need
to write it down.

Visiting Friends

Good people and bad people. The ones who are bad are bad to
themselves, bad in nuance, bad over time, bad in the poles
around which

error writhes, obviously
ouroboros,
collecting.

Old friends and ones I never knew
I know them now. A trip

to visit, motiveless, *why are you here, I don't understand. But I
will make you*

comfortable.
The ones in compromised

relationships, unrepeatable dependencies, the ones

at the start of long collaborations about which it is impossible

not to be starry-eyed

stars get in your eyes in their domain
necrotic definition.

Thoughtful
grocery shopping.

Younger people know less about themselves, in general, but only
for the moment, they will learn and then forget. They all have
blind spots, and some of these are larger than others. Some have
large eyes only on one side.

The good people, they turn bad, and they turn good, they come
to grips and they turn a cold eye and a warm one. The visitor is
no judge, sees it all, skewers, valorizes, vivisection, "Jackie,"

a pseudonym. Jackie and her husband Jake, driven and wired,
their little daughters, 6 and ten, fierce and sad, the fierce one
    happy and the sad one angry—the rivalry between them in
    their pajamas Saturday morning so intense
minutiae hour by hour the clock of who got what and how much
    they will not relinquish,
they mince their days.

I can see the problem (Motherlove) and name its solution
    (Motherlove). There is no self from which to issue to self
a prohibition. There is a peevish
father with recourse to bench, to seat, to sin

—some good
some bad

moral ambiguity he could never
handle

performative, some people
diminutive, others
restrained, hesitant, forward thinking,
difficult to reach

he tried to write about it
he wrote about it like a robot writes about
moral ambiguity

like a robot
likes data

have you ever seen
fabricated
moral ambiguity?
It's painful to look at
painful to watch

it doesn't make you uncomfortable
like moral ambiguity should

when it's good.

++

I see good people and bad people

on my trip. I don't discriminate
and stop with them all

a thoughtful guest and I pile up
my towels, the dirty ones, I don't need privacy or company.
   Neither

must you accompany me nor leave me be, neither give me
      space nor
hold my hand. The clean ones

I fold and stack. Clean
pillowcases I leave
on the pillows, catch my drift. The pillowcase

with a faint
imprint of my hot new
snake tattoo, life-size, prominent   supine
my right arm, I crumple and drop on the floor. Snake

on, or in, my right arm, the difference between a thought
and its imprint on time, in time the thought had attached to it
an action

serpent of decision

snake of mistake

Snake of self   snake of other: snake of self and other. Snake
    in residence

on my arm: I awoke in basement quarters, quiet, square, and
    dim, and in a full-length mirror was afraid of my new
    tattoo. Frightened by. Prima imago

remember you are not you and so not

to be held accountable not responsible there's no self there to
    do anything on anyone forever. Motherlove

no substitute. The fierce happy daughter misspoke the snake's
    name as Mischief. Misnomer, Miss Malaprop.

Jackie and Jake bring me to a busy party at a happy home, an
A-frame multilevel home with unpainted wood everywhere, and
shrubs. Lots of people and children, including one from another
planet. As long as the mom remembers the girl came from
another planet things go better, her daughter slides habitually
down the basement steps, head first, she slaps herself and
doesn't speak, eats liquid through a gastric feeding tube. Her
mom and dad met on this planet, they are in love with each other
and support each other and maintain their humor. In public kiss
and caress. They are wry and sleep-deprived.

Oh and there's Dan, his wife Sadie, their son Milo. Their huge dog. Old sweetheart, he fell in love with me, indelibly, painting pumpkins silver on the porch, October sunshaft. Stopping by with my long arm wrapped in Saran and a greasy bleeding etching of a snake, I unwrap it, don't want to scare Milo, but he takes it in, says he likes it. What is an adult with a giant

snake lying

formidable, it is not meant to amuse children. What does a
    child do with
materia
matter of the adult that detaches

and reaches out a self-imposed wound
jetsam of the realm that flutters down from atmospheric
    height
trace material unmeant

insoluble
turn an eye—

Sadie has big feet like me, I leave with a bag of high-end
shoes and boots that fit me better

like her husband fits me better
I don't want to scare Milo

What is a metaphor if not a simile.

What is a tattoo if not the mark of impermanence
I wear it on my sleeve
There's a thousand other ways I could have done this snake
No that's stupid
There's
a million other ways
there's thousands and trillions, infinity ways
I could have done this snake
but I had to choose
or I had to choose not to do it
Not to do this snake

Snake of decision
snake of mistake
snake of decision
rammed up my spine
snake in my yin
snake in my yang

I should have got the skin
not the snake
the skin

    ++

Is there anyone I am forgetting

Sister-mate of misery, I will not expose thee

Onerous habit of doing what I please
Nun-like crone, wife of relinquishment
Castaway drapery of habitué
Stop here no longer
Hie thee

to the sauna of the hermitage
fortified domicile where stooping man and mousetrap wife
and twin progeny
live lives like locks

—these marriages, they look to me like knots
to be untied

the shapes in the tiles: squares or rectangles
peace in the deep bath
dark wood finishing the windows

I used to think that I was a metaphor for you.
But where does that leave you.

Another man and wife unremarked in the most conscious
harmony: she knows herself, and he knows her. Her frailties are
her character, the bones of her. He built a house for her. Why
question it? What is superior

in self-reliance? If it is superior, it is unexistent. Is there any-
thing wrong in how much she thrives, supported, hydroponic

vine climbing inside with the long blinds drawn against blue de-
sert sunshine?

Culminating in San Francisco: apartment in the Presidio—

inhabitants mellow, calm and fruitful
second lives working out just fine despite the daughter left
    behind in Paris—

where I sleep still moving in my dream body
sixteen hours slamming on the 5 in the white Yaris

and Martin and me
we have caught up so thoroughly
old friend sleeping platonically in bed
after bed we hardly
ever have to make our own beds we just lie in them,
back home he has a laugh with Wendy, calls
her frequently, so frequently it drives me crazy,
would drive me crazy to call
or be called,
be called upon to call. Thirteen meals with Martin in

complete agreement
tandem

detachable

friend
ouroboros there is no end
snake at the end

some of that continuity
there's some of that continuity you've all been wanting
you've been looking for
there's some of that continuity you've all been looking for.

"As long as I get to be with you at the end"

6

Shame on you for thinking people can't change

I sucked my boyfriend's cock this morning like a champ

a bit estranged
yet ready and responsive

come what may they

can do they
can do they can

do they
do they
do.

If I wanted something exquisite

for my home
where would I turn

to whom shall I apply

something to look at
all day long

should I choose to spend the entire day
at home

in bespoke
stratosphere

—something in the way—

between light
and me

a socialite

outline of a peasant
outlines of something useful

put me
in the way

between it
and its silhouette

muslin's drape
object's placement

with regard
and in relation

to the source of light. I'm having a leisurely

or strenuous time
in pursuit of Bloomsbury

ergonomics the hot heart of
craftsmanship

it's all so
well made

flat plane mounted
on a plinth that frames
a hearth

outcroppings of
coterie

stone-cold
community

the nucleus of crushed

velvet
refinery

terms used by tradesmen

—cutouts of tradesmen—

darling children
—cutouts of children—
the auto-

didactic
unlimited

inborn
apprehension they are born

clients

with strong
preferences

not scholars and certainly
not curators
or makers.

Dear Jen

I write

to apologize for my poorly timed critique of gentrification, capitalism. Tom's new shop Valley Variety announces an exhibition of your paintings, vibrant amongst dun-colored retail made by local artisans and international product designers. I came inside your house to pick up my share of our share from the farm, this is not the time. I know you spent a lot of time inside that space, yesterday, hanging your show, and Proprietor Tom helped you do it—good attention to detail, which is important to you; I know you well enough to know how important. If you were really my friend—I miss you—I miss—would I write to you in this public space? I intended to write a real letter to you, began composing it in my head, and then saw the space in which it really lived.

+++

Dear Jen

Is it possible to launch a critique

from inside—stay inside

Valley Variety

nowhere to put that

Ready Smile, a
ready smile
trained on light source, the refraction a nonspecific
obliteration

everything only connected by [ ] and [ ]
that's a poem I HEART

but these are not the poles
I meant or set out to

and if you find a warm vein stay in the
bath of blood
it's cold on the outside
of the feeling of being inside

pragmatism to hang back
dangle auto-
eros
on a hook or strap it lets you

hate and restrain.
Inside collaboration
is content. Experience of. Changed by. Outside, to snark
   completely, is self-
"Congratulations, you collaborated."

bloodbath, to make my meaning clear, in company,
can you get inside the perimeter I love you like

myself; I love you like I love myself; I hate you like I hate
    myself

and guess what hired by out-
'n'-out nepotism—so what—within the structure it's like
so what; ends and means there is no better way, determinism of
the "Circle"—get yourself inside of that. Get your brain around
that circle and stay inside, it's warmer there, in company. Mon-
ster,

glistening in blood-fluid that is killing and borning

rest inside at last. Sincere applause. I write

to apologize

    +++

And another thing, Jen, I think I'm done with monogamy,
    crap product of capital, I come inside
your converted farmhouse, tidy and cozy, sweet Rachel at the
    Singer
1947 plying her rosy skills to make a canopy
for your bed

and I arrive renegade, awful, a seamstress ripping out

hems deconstructing
patterns sewing on backwards and did I really mean it, do I doubt

myself again, can I make a solid critique, is there a position from
which I can stand inside
"your warm and cozy house"
your love
meanwhile

that man

I sewed his coat for him
I paid his bills for him I gave him
a set of keys and bought bread and bananas and yogurt
for him but all he wanna tell me now is Do I own you
and Did you fuck him, make you mine, I need to know, he talks
    like I signed away or he talks like he wants me to

sign away

Whyn't you go down to Florida and look for your daddy

I'll release blood like the virgin Mary

on your departure you could find

the Slit

The rush   to ruin
headlong

Slim line
of shoulder   neck

Whyn't you jerk yourself off
sure and slow
build up
I'll watch

Can you see from outside how sick I am—the feeling of not
    being well is vacuous
Can you see how sick I am inside—it's like a shadow play,
    procedurally   the way
I have to knock-

knock on this head—

come in, projection—

knock on that head

cum in a tissue, ritual,

ritual. Life of

quiet study.

How do you objectify the day

look at that little nose

twitching
over a little orificial—

is it eating itself—that's a joke—

you are going to make me ruin it
if you force me to talk about it,

a poetics of being ornery and delimited—oh no, I got this far
    without accommodating you;
a poetics of being comic about the distance between us—a
    comedy in which you're everyone

and I'm me

Look at this bra.
(It's a pill)
Look with me, at this bra.

Look at the cats, cleaning
themselves. I love how they

bathe at the same time even though they are not
in the same place.

But I can see
them
both.

Let me take a measurement—
no, just eyeball it.

Your arms are long
your torso, narrow, I can

eyeball that on the hanger

and tell you it will fit you
and buy it for you. That's how much

You are perfect for me

because you're psychic
no one else could understand me
the way you

do and

I say
Drink Me

I say it to you silently
but it calls forth in me

the water for you
the water you asked for

Was It Hubris

I wore that giant talisman
Ebony
Brass Inlay
Shaker Tree of Life

Was it perfection that allowed it

found by me—I find the best things, I have such a good

eye, but my mouth, my mouth

is a "dirty whore," accordingly, and in my mouth foul
language, craven

invitations. I lost it.

Take offense, young
officer: You were approaching my mouth with
an instrument

called a "torch"
you were stretching my lower
lip to the limit with a gloved

index, forcing
my jaw to endurance
forcing my jaw to patience, hinge, protract

you forced me to this base kind of poem
with the viscera.

Young Man with Instrument
dirty words "dirty whore" in connection
with my mouth   SWAK

your cock hitting my face

A long time ago   in a different
sort of poem   I said "nothing

purple comes near the face"   NEVER
say never

for what of this morning
glory deviating
from perfection of
solipsism
decadence
inversion morning
glory of the blue? What of the

deviant from nature. Words he said was

"dirty whore"

no one ever called me that

before.

It's like kissing a dead man

on a gurney, that close to walking

only charred phoenix

rising from the ashes
of the relative

these recurrent themes
kept me measuring—the external—

wailing on a plank
a dead dog on a stick
wailing

like a dead
mother.

He's so beautiful in his fugue

he's so beautiful, the slant—
the shaft

reclined—
abandoned—

it was worth all

      the dying. He wakes up—in the sun shaft, on the plank
opens his eyes—

"it's going to be okay
yr smart and pretty
and people like you"

That's what the dead man say.

Why I am not a Buddhist

"effortless"

compassion for history

is faith, just like if I

accepted Jesus, my Savior, like I tattoo'd my chest with the
    Number,

the Beast. It's hard to choose a name. Choose compassion

for Self that is not magical—it didn't have to be this way

I made it this way—But that's

okay. I'm okay

You're okay: historically

shown

to be true: That is love that is

Compassion. Compassion

for the lost and the wandering, the learning

and the Mythic: Within my personal mythos

an ethos of lost heartlessness—preserve

that carnal sense of one's alonelessness
the light of no dependent
the light of inviolation

—vaginally I might

orgasm if I can feel you, really

feel you, mimetically

what you are feeling of me, you let your impassioned breathing

ream my eardrum, timbre in tympanum. I wake up frightened

that you are the person in the world

closest to me; all others maintain their constellate

forms; I will have to educate you to my diffuse needs by means
    of the tender arts

of cinema and poetry.

Wizard of the Western World

and just like that

it's okay for me to pull a rabbit

out of a hat

it's not okay for you to heft it

skin and bones

boil it

stringy meat

in your poor white teeth

Start a Book

I used to have nothing to write about

yet anyway I wrote

now with the manger full of hangry
beasts, gums bared in the night

haggard error in my belt
whipping commencing

laterally
bilaterally
unilaterally

your sincerity pales
beside my insincerity.

+

He told me the shock had not yet
worn off—I just thought it had but it had not
nearly. I was still
in shock.

Did I make you laugh? I said:
What does not kill us makes us strong: Discuss. It's a middle-

class problem, things happening for a reason. The journey
of life, the need for god's

o'ershadowing hand
to wipe,
to scoop. I need it now

   +

that's why I write
so, I write so

to put some of that throne energy
into practice

put your enemy
on a throne and bring him

from far off the gifts of fruit foreign
to his lips

bring him the colors he's never seen
azure the name of the

longest day he never lived in your love you never
gave to him.

   +

I love these (stretched) feelings
of the fucked legs

How many (everywhere) can you say you love?

Here's a song I don't know
I don't know what's going to happen with you and me, babe

Formerly I would just read anything—

all the learning from texts
tangential material how

Rumanian peasantry
slaughter their pigs
cook their noodles—

as long as it's well written

    +

haven't finished it yet—
don't finish it.

It's a high-class thing, in the higher classes you can do anything
you need

to meet your needs
ask me to say I love you

up here appetite shuts down when death in-
stinct

rears
tall as a man
wide as your throat.

    +

I hate the way you close
the shades it's so
low class

I hate the way you lower
your voice it's so middle-
class

at tables in
restaurants
and cafes. If you wait long enough

and try hard enough
you will get into it,
the book. Anywhere you are
it is possible to become absorbed

in your reading.

Ant Life

She is a great host.
She keeps

largely
to herself. Keys to herself. A host

inviolate keeps
that beast in the castle
who hides

his yonder
ugliness

politely. When I have need

dig in
drink deep. She lies

dimly
sonorously

generous
does not do her justice

she has evacuated

for me

the premises.
The premise is

she does enough
she is enough
the pronoun *she*

distracts from her
genus

detracts from her
genius

SO GOOD
TOO KIND

ANT LICE
life

of the mind.

Acknowledgments

Thank you to some readers and encouragers. Joshua Beckman, Betsy Bonner, Caroline Crumpacker, Matthew Dickman, Emily Wallis Hughes, Lucy Ives, Cate Marvin, Ariana Reines, Kenneth Reveiz, Adam Ross, Kendra Sullivan, Cathy Wagner, Pamela Wolff.